T0082930

Endorsements

In a world that prizes fame, success, and wealth, it's vital to stay focused on the one and only thing that can truly bring meaning -- our relationship with God. Matthew takes us on a thought-provoking journey in *A Meaningless Devotion* that will challenge and encourage you as you pursue a life of meaning.

Shawn Lovejoy,
Founder and CEO of <u>CourageToLead.com</u>

In today's society we are constantly shown our differences. This world tells us to put our needs first, grab all we can of the material wealth and retreat to our corners to enjoy the spoils of our gains. It truly is a meaningless approach that pulls us away from God's love, Grace and plan for each of us. A Meaningless Devotional is a series of biblical reminders that the passionate pursuit of God will lead to spiritual wealth. As I personally face the challenges of being in Congress, I find the Day 10 devotion a good reminder of how important it is to come together as a body of believers in our spiritual journey. Ecclesiastes 4:9-12 tells us that two are better than one. it confirms that we are stronger and safer together than as an individual. In a world that pulls us away from God, we should bind together as a body of faith to guard against the illusion of satisfaction that the secular tempts us with.

A. Drew Ferguson IV, DMD

MEANING(LESS)
DEVOTIONAL

MATTHEW S. THROWER

WESTBOW
PRESS®
A DIVISION OF THOMAS NELSON
& ZONDERVAN

Copyright © 2018 Matthew S. Thrower.

All rights reserved. No part of this book may be used or reproduced by
any means, graphic, electronic, or mechanical, including photocopying,
recording, taping or by any information storage retrieval system
without the written permission of the author except in the case of
brief quotations embodied in critical articles and reviews.

This book is a work of non-fiction. Unless otherwise noted, the author
and the publisher make no explicit guarantees as to the accuracy of
the information contained in this book and in some cases, names of
people and places have been altered to protect their privacy.

Scripture quotations are from the ESV® Bible (The Holy Bible, English
Standard Version®), copyright © 2001 by Crossway, a publishing ministry
of Good News Publishers. Used by permission. All rights reserved.

WestBow Press books may be ordered through booksellers or by contacting:

WestBow Press
A Division of Thomas Nelson & Zondervan
1663 Liberty Drive
Bloomington, IN 47403
www.westbowpress.com
1 (866) 928-1240

Because of the dynamic nature of the Internet, any web addresses or
links contained in this book may have changed since publication and
may no longer be valid. The views expressed in this work are solely those
of the author and do not necessarily reflect the views of the publisher,
and the publisher hereby disclaims any responsibility for them.

Any people depicted in stock imagery provided by Thinkstock are models,
and such images are being used for illustrative purposes only.
Certain stock imagery © Thinkstock.

ISBN: 978-1-9736-1273-5 (sc)
ISBN: 978-1-9736-1274-2 (e)

Library of Congress Control Number: 2017919756

Print information available on the last page.

WestBow Press rev. date: 01/18/2018

*To anyone who is on an adventure to find
meaning for his or her life.*

Acknowledgements

I want to thank my wife and children for their endless love for me, God and life. You guys have stood by me and my God-given vision to see a glimpse of God's kingdom touchdown in our world. I never feel like I'm doing this alone because I have you guys by my side. I'm also forever grateful to my Refuge Point Church family for listening to my "Meaningless" sermons through the book of Ecclesiastes. You guys are the greatest group of people on earth! Thanks for helping me keep our church meaningful in our community. Finally, I have to say a huge thank you to Carrie Busch. Because of your help, this dream became a reality.

A Meaningless Introduction

Most in our society desire success and wealth. This desire drives our thinking-- we want more success, more money, and we expect that nothing bad should ever happen to us. However, the Bible runs counter to this thinking. God's definition of success is made plain in five consecutive books known as the Wisdom Literature (Job, Psalms, Proverbs, Ecclesiastes, and Song of Solomon) in the middle of the Old Testament. The Wisdom Literature contains narratives of individual lives.

Proverbs is a field guide for how we can define and achieve success in our individual lives. Next, Psalms mostly contains the writings of the great king, David, who experiences some major emotional ups and downs. In a moment of desperation, he cries out, "How long, Oh Lord, will You forget me forever?" and then only a few lines later, he tells us, "I will sing to the Lord, because he has dealt bountifully with me." (Psalm 13) David is so relatable for me, so I understand his writings very well. Then, you have Song of Solomon, a book about the celebration of sex.

Job and Ecclesiastes are two books that seem to form one lesson, despite being on two opposite sides of the spectrum. Job is a wealthy and godly man, and the devil strikes him with boils. So, Job sits in ashes, completely poor with dogs licking his wounds, and arrives at the end of all of this by saying, "Naked I came from my mother's womb, and naked shall I return. The Lord gave and the Lord has taken away; blessed be the name of the Lord." (Job 1:21)

Most of us can't say we have suffered like Job. Yet, we still complain: "If I had more money, if I had more power, if I had more friends, if I had better religion, then life would be better." What we desire is an unrealistic existence.

The focus of this 45-Day Devotional is Ecclesiastes, which also deals with our desire for meaning and our perspective of success. In this book, we learn:

1) Don't take yourself too seriously
2) Don't waste your life on materialism
3) God is the only way to find meaning

With that, King Solomon allows us to lean in on an adventure to discover all that is under heaven. He was the wisest, most powerful, and wealthiest man at that time. During his adventure of finding meaning, he finds that everything under the sun is "meaningless"… and that true meaning is only found over the sun, in God.

Ecclesiastes 1:1-3
The words of the Preacher, the son of David, king in Jerusalem.
Vanity of vanities, says the Preacher, vanity of vanities! All is vanity.
What does man gain by all the toil at which he toils under the sun?

Talk about an introduction! Meaningless! Meaningless!
(That's how the word, "vanity" translates – from the word
vapor or *a puff of air, fleeting or illusive*). It seriously sounds like
the Preacher (whom most people believe is Solomon) needs
a warm hug from a snowman. I actually love the direct tone
he sets and how quick he is to point out that everything is
meaningless. At the forefront of this book, he points to the
fact that if God is not in the center of your activities, then your
activities are meaningless.

Solomon is direct because he has experienced both life on the
mountain and life in the ghetto, and has found that all of his
experiences were meaningless. When all is said and done and
when you breathe your last breath, will your life have been
meaningful or meaningless?

Solomon doesn't waste any time in this book either. He's quick to point out that everything is meaningless and you're just stuck in a never-ending cycle. It reminds me of that commercial that says, "Your life is like a treadmill." That's exactly what the writer is comparing our lives to. In other words, no matter how hard you work, there's always something else to work on. It's like doing laundry. No matter how many times you wash your clothes, you're going to have to rewash them and go through the cycle all over again. Pun intended.

In verse 3, he tosses in the word *toil,* which means "to labor until the point of exhaustion and experience little reward." I have often been guilty of working on things that I know wouldn't bring any reward or satisfaction. In fact, I often find myself working on something that I have no business working on at all. I think Solomon's point is that things will only change when we start working for God's glory and walking in the purpose He has for us. Hard work is not meaningless when you are doing it for His glory, nor is it meaningless if it is according to the will of God. Life and work are meaningless only when they are self-serving. If we could slow down from the treadmill of life, we'd come to the same conclusion as Solomon; without God at the center of our activities, life is meaningless.

Ecclesiastes 1:4-11

A generation goes, and a generation comes, but the earth remains forever. The sun rises, and the sun goes down, and hastens to the place where it rises. The wind blows to the south and goes around to the north; around and around goes the wind, and on its circuits the wind returns. All streams run to the sea, but the sea is not full; to the place where the streams flow, there they flow again. All things are full of weariness; a man cannot utter it; the eye is not satisfied with seeing, nor the ear filled with hearing. What has been is what will be, and what has been done is what will be done, and there is nothing new under the sun. Is there a thing of which it is said, "See, this is new"? It has been already in the ages before us. There is no remembrance of former things, nor will there be any remembrance of later things yet to be among those who come after.

There have been plenty of powerful human forces in our history, but the writer wants to point out that no human force is as powerful as the force of nature. Mankind is strong and the force of the Jedi is even stronger, but they are nothing compared to the force of nature. Yet, even nature is limited in what it can do in an attempt to change the world. Why?

Because it is controlled by God and only God can change the world.

Solomon was intrigued by the fact that humans have come and gone, but nature has primarily stayed the same. There seemed to be change everywhere, yet nothing was really changing.

Through what he has presented to us thus far, we are left with this pressing question: is there anything new under the sun? My answer may be "yes" if I lived in Ancient Israel; however, since I am surrounded by modern science, it is difficult to see the world as unchanging. See, we are living in a time where keeping up with the latest trends in cars, design, fashion, and technology is exhausting. The only problem is that our pursuit of toys and trinkets will leave us hungry for more.

People often flock to new sights and sounds, only to find that these things won't satisfy them. We all try to fill an empty void in our life with something transient; yet, in the end, we find that it is meaningless. The writer is declaring a central truth of all Scripture-- that all things exist by God and for God. Without this view of life, nothing has real meaning. Without God, life is futile and meaningless.

3

Ecclesiastes 1:12-18

I the Preacher have been king over Israel in Jerusalem. And I applied my heart to seek and to search out by wisdom all that is done under heaven. It is an unhappy business that God has given to the children of man to be busy with. I have seen everything that is done under the sun, and behold, all is vanity and a striving after wind. What is crooked cannot be made straight, and what is lacking cannot be counted. I said in my heart, "I have acquired great wisdom, surpassing all who were over Jerusalem before me, and my heart has had great experience of wisdom and knowledge." And I applied my heart to know wisdom and to know madness and folly. I perceived that this also is but a striving after wind. For in much wisdom is much vexation, and he who increases knowledge increases sorrow.

Solomon was on a journey to have understanding of (literally) everything under the sun. Even though he couldn't understand everything, his ultimate conclusion was that everything is meaningless and a "striving after the wind." As part of this journey, he also sought to understand foolishness and stupid behavior, which he found led to a wasted life. Think about when you have foolishly trusted in your own understanding and ultimately failed. The more we rely on our own understanding, the more sorrow it will cause.

Solomon took the road of luxury, marbled all he had, and encrusted it in gold. He ate the finest meals and drank the finest wine. He partied like it was 1999. After he had acquired all that stuff and did all the things that the rich did, he decided that it was meaningless. So, he found some rednecks in Alabama and hung out with them. After he found himself drunk from cheap whiskey in the back of a beat up Ford Ranger, he found that it was also meaningless. Either road, whether luxurious or impoverished, does not have meaning without God.

Everyone knows that something just seems off in our world-- that there is something that is broken and no matter how we try to fix it, we are stuck on the treadmill of life. The diagnosis is that we need someone beyond the sun to fix the brokenness. The remedy is Jesus. Through Jesus, we find our meaning "under heaven." Only when we follow Jesus will we start living life to see everything "over heaven" kiss everything "under heaven." Living life in the moment will cause our lives to be void of meaning; however, a life lived for the Kingdom of God brings meaning not only to us, but to those around us.

4

Ecclesiastes 2:1-11

I said in my heart, "Come now, I will test you with pleasure; enjoy yourself." But behold, this also was vanity. I said of laughter, "It is mad," and of pleasure, "What use is it?" I searched with my heart how to cheer my body with wine—my heart still guiding me with wisdom—and how to lay hold on folly, till I might see what was good for the children of man to do under heaven during the few days of their life. I made great works. I built houses and planted vineyards for myself. I made myself gardens and parks, and planted in them all kinds of fruit trees. I made myself pools from which to water the forest of growing trees. I bought male and female slaves, and had slaves who were born in my house. I had also great possessions of herds and flocks, more than any who had been before me in Jerusalem. I also gathered for myself silver and gold and the treasure of kings and provinces. I got singers, both men and women, and many concubines, the delight of the sons of man. So I became great and surpassed all who were before me in Jerusalem. Also my wisdom remained with me. And whatever my eyes desired I did not keep from them. I kept my heart from no pleasure, for my heart found pleasure in all my toil, and this was my reward for all my toil. Then I considered all that my hands had done and the toil I had expended in doing it, and behold, all was vanity and a striving after wind, and there was nothing to be gained under the sun.

Solomon's efforts to be both wise and foolish achieved nothing. So, what about pleasure? In Ecclesiastes 2, Solomon begins to live a life of hedonism (which is a fancy word for *pleasure* or *self-indulgence*).

We all have a thirst to please ourselves, but in the end, the pleasures of the world will leave us unquenched. Finding meaning in pleasure is the equivalent to drawing from a well full of sand. It will never satisfy us. Solomon found that his pursuit of pleasure was also meaningless. Thus, our only hope is to draw from the living well that comes from Jesus. Jesus is the only One who can satisfy our thirst.

Solomon was the Bill Gates of his time. In fact, his wealth far exceeded Bill Gates to the tune of what some believe was $2.1 trillion. Verses 4-8 begins to tell us some of the things Solomon did for his own pleasure. His parties were far more extravagant than anything we have ever seen. Since downloading music to his iPhone wasn't good enough, he would buy the band. Women were at his beck and call. He built forests, vineyards, parks, houses-- everything you can imagine. Some scholars believe that he was throwing parties for up to 15,000 people a day. If he saw something he wanted, he got it. Yet, what did he get for all his toil?

He experienced fleeting pleasure. Solomon played as hard as he could and ended up just how he started: bored.

Similarly, our culture is hedonistic. We will go to great lengths and get into enormous amounts of debt to temporarily escape the crushing realities of life. The truth is that we are more like Solomon than we realize. We chase after new toys and trinkets, thinking that they will leave us happy and fulfilled. In the end, like Solomon, we will find that it is meaningless.

Have you ever struggled with trying to find satisfaction and fulfillment in "things" and "pleasure"? Where do you go to quench your thirst? If it's not Jesus, then you'll find that it's all meaningless.

Ecclesiastes 2:12-27

So I turned to consider wisdom and madness and folly. For what can the man do who comes after the king? Only what has already been done. Then I saw that there is more gain in wisdom than in folly, as there is more gain in light than in darkness. The wise person has his eyes in his head, but the fool walks in darkness. And yet I perceived that the same event happens to all of them. Then I said in my heart, "What happens to the fool will happen to me also. Why then have I been so very wise?" And I said in my heart that this also is vanity. For of the wise as of the fool there is no enduring remembrance, seeing that in the days to come all will have been long forgotten. How the wise dies just like the fool! So I hated life, because what is done under the sun was grievous to me, for all is vanity and a striving after wind.

We now turn to the harsh reality of death. We find Solomon lamenting and asking, "What good is wisdom, wealth, and pleasure if you are going to end up being painted like a clown - buried six feet under ground?".

Thanks for the reminder, Solomon.

Being prepared for death doesn't remove the burden of life from Solomon. It takes a long time for a person to learn how to live, and then BAAM! Life is over. When Solomon said that he "hated life," I think he was saying that he was disgusted with its futility. What is the sense in living if there is no meaning?

Jesus said in John 10:10, "The thief comes only to steal, kill and destroy. I [Jesus] came that they may have life and have it abundantly." As Christians, we have been given the green light to love life. We are to put everything we have into it and get the most out of it for the glory of God. We may not enjoy everything about life, but with Jesus our lives have purpose and meaning.

How can you pour more energy in to having the abundant life that Jesus said we should have?

Day

6

Ecclesiastes 2:18-26

I hated all my toil in which I toil under the sun, seeing that I must leave it to the man who will come after me, and who knows whether he will be wise or a fool? Yet he will be master of all for which I toiled and used my wisdom under the sun. This also is vanity. So I turned about and gave my heart up to despair over all the toil of my labors under the sun, because sometimes a person who has toiled with wisdom and knowledge and skill must leave everything to be enjoyed by someone who did not toil for it. This also is vanity and a great evil. What has a man from all the toil and striving of heart with which he toils beneath the sun? For all his days are full of sorrow, and his work is a vexation. Even in the night his heart does not rest. This also is vanity. There is nothing better for a person than that he should eat and drink and find enjoyment in his toil. This also, I saw, is from the hand of God, for apart from him who can eat or who can have enjoyment? For to the one who pleases him God has given wisdom and knowledge and joy, but to the sinner he has given the business of gathering and collecting, only to give to one who pleases God. This also is vanity and a striving after wind.

At this point, Solomon sounds depressed. Not only does he *hate* his life (see yesterday's devotion on his use of the word *hate*), but he also hates his money, simply because he has to leave it to someone else when he dies and he fears that person may waste it. Cry me a river. Right?

Solomon, however, is making a valid point that for all of the labor that goes into making money, what do we gain? In the end, we die and can't take it with us. As the saying goes, "The U-Haul doesn't follow the hearse."

What matters is how we steward our money while we are alive. We have the obligation to enjoy our money by using it for God's glory. Are you using your money for the glory of God? Are you using your money to advance the Kingdom of God? Or are you wasting it on living a meaningless life, chasing after your selfish desires?

Solomon concludes this section in Ecclesiastes in an interesting way. We need to think carefully about what Solomon is saying in these final verses of this section. Solomon is not advocating for us to "Eat, drink, and be merry!" Rather, he is saying that we ought to thank God for all we have and use it for His glory. All of the blessings that we have are from God and we ought to use them for His glory, for those who don't are considered evil.

When God is at the center of everything we do, life has purpose and meaning. Life, death, wisdom and wealth are all in God's hands. Apart from God, there can be no true enjoyment in these things. Apart from God, everything is meaningless. *Vanities of vanities,* says the preacher.

Hold Up, Broseph!

As you prepare for Ecclesiastes Chapter 3, consider the following: Our view of God is going to hold huge significance as we continue our study. Knowing God seems like it's a tall order, but as we study the Bible we find that He reveals His character and attributes. The Bible does not teach that God is a fairy, a genie in a bottle, or a weak old man. Rather, the Bible reveals that God is sovereign, all powerful, all knowing, is at all places at all times, and is in complete control over every situation. Nothing surprises Him and He governs even in the chaotic times of life.

So, as we talk about the seasons of life that Solomon is going to outline, we will find there is someone [God] above who is in complete control and is balancing our life's experiences. Knowing this should bring rest to our souls. Whatever season you find yourself in, know that God loves you and is working everything out for your good and for His glory.

Day

7

Ecclesiastes 3:1-15

For everything there is a season, and a time for every matter under heaven: a time to be born, and a time to die; a time to plant, and a time to pluck up what is planted; a time to kill, and a time to heal; a time to break down, and a time to build up; a time to weep, and a time to laugh; a time to mourn, and a time to dance; a time to cast away stones, and a time to gather stones together; a time to embrace, and a time to refrain from embracing; a time to seek, and a time to lose; a time to keep, and a time to cast away; a time to tear, and a time to sew; a time to keep silence, and a time to speak; a time to love, and a time to hate; a time for war, and a time for peace. What gain has the worker from his toil? I have seen the business that God has given to the children of man to be busy with. He has made everything beautiful in its time. Also, he has put eternity into man's heart, yet so that he cannot find out what God has done from the beginning to the end. I perceived that there is nothing better for them than to be joyful and to do good as long as they live; also that everyone should eat and drink and take pleasure in all his toil—this is God's gift to man. I perceived that whatever God does endures forever; nothing can be added to it, nor anything taken from it. God has done it, so that people fear before him. That which is, already has been; that which is to be, already has been; and God seeks what has been driven away.

No – the Byrds song, "Turn, Turn, Turn," didn't make this passage popular. Solomon wrote this passage thousands of years prior to 1965, and has been read by millions prior to the Byrds famous song. (Although it is a really good song.)

Everything that happens, the good and bad and the small and big, is in God's appropriate time. No matter who you are, you know that "times and seasons" are a regular part of life. Every season, even the bad, is beautiful because it flows with the plan of God.

Yet, none of us WANT to experience the bad seasons. They sound much nicer in written form than they play out in real life. I only want the good times. I like birth, planting, building up, dancing, laughing, speaking, and loving, but I don't like death, breaking down, weeping, mourning, tearing down, silence, and war. The only problem is that we can't pick which season we are in.

If Solomon said in verse 11, "He has made everything beautiful in its time" then we can rest in the fact that it also includes the difficulties of life. In other words, there is a purpose behind every season in life. It is God's plan to make EVERYTHING beautiful in its time, which means every trial, tear, heartache, and suffering will be beautiful in the end.

It's also important for us to never grow envious of other people's prosperous seasons they are in. Never get too anxious to get to the next season of life either. If you can find God in the season that you are in, you will find that everything doesn't happen for a reason; rather, everything happens for God's reason. If we surrender to God and His timing, life will go from meaningless to meaningful.

8

Ecclesiastes 3:16-22

Moreover, I saw under the sun that in the place of justice, even there was wickedness, and in the place of righteousness, even there was wickedness. I said in my heart, God will judge the righteous and the wicked, for there is a time for every matter and for every work. I said in my heart with regard to the children of man that God is testing them that they may see that they themselves are but beasts. For what happens to the children of man and what happens to the beasts is the same; as one dies, so dies the other. They all have the same breath, and man has no advantage over the beasts, for all is vanity. All go to one place. All are from the dust, and to dust all return. Who knows whether the spirit of man goes upward and the spirit of the beast goes down into the earth? So I saw that there is nothing better than that a man should rejoice in his work, for that is his lot. Who can bring him to see what will be after him?

If at the end of our day there is nothing, then life is meaningless. If this world is all there is, then we are living a futile life. However, since there is a God who loves us, life is meaningful. All of our heartache becomes purposeful. One of the fundamental points the preacher is making throughout the book of Ecclesiastes is that, without God, life is meaningless and only God can make sense of all the chaos in the world. Today's passage reveals this truth. With all of the brokenness, injustice, and futility in this world, it is hard to make sense of everything.

In this passage, Solomon again examines life's "vanities." It seems like he compares us to Sasquatch when he says, "the children of man are beasts." Yeah, I don't think so. This passage does not mean what you may think. Solomon is saying that at the end of our life we will turn to dust just like all of the beasts, Sasquatches, and animals of the earth. (Side note: I don't believe in Sasquatch, but my father and oldest son seems to think differently.)

So, how should we live life knowing that we will go to the grave no less than the beasts? How do we live life knowing that there will always be injustice in this world? Solomon suggests that we live life in the present. We are to live life to the fullest and enjoy what God has given us today. We should try not to concern ourselves with the worries of tomorrow lest we miss God moving in our present reality.

We ought to drink in deeply the joys of this life knowing that, one day, we will be in a never-ending fountain of joy in the presence of God.

I am convinced that this chapter is one of the most popular chapters in the Old Testament for a good reason. It reveals the harsh reality of life, yet at the same time gives us the hope that we have a loving God with us at all times. Solomon concludes this chapter by telling us to enjoy the season that

God has placed us in today. Whatever season that is, find joy and peace.

If you are not in a rough season of life, I encourage you to find someone who is and reach out to him or her with love. This is what we are supposed to be doing as believers in Jesus. If you are in a tough season where trauma is reigning, I want to tell you three things: 1) **God is with you**. I know that is the cliché thing to say, but this is the hope we have. Knowing that God is with us helps us to place our hope on the eternal as opposed to what is temporal. 2) **Find someone to help.** I know that sounds crazy, but when I am experiencing trauma in my life, helping people actually helps me deal with my situations with a clearer perspective. 3) **Find other Christian's to do life with.** We are better when we have others who will go through the storms of life with us.

Ecclesiastes 4:1-6

Again, I observed all the oppression that takes place under the sun. I saw the tears of the oppressed, with no one to comfort them. The oppressors have great power, and their victims are helpless. So I concluded that the dead are better off than the living. But most fortunate of all are those who are not yet born. For they have not seen all the evil that is done under the sun. Then I observed that most people are motivated to success because they envy their neighbors. But this, too, is meaningless—like chasing the wind. "Fools fold their idle hands, leading them to ruin." And yet, "Better to have one handful with quietness than two handfuls with hard work and chasing the wind."

In chapter 4, Solomon gives us the "why" behind the "what" of belonging to a community of believers. Before we dive deep in this chapter, it's important for us to have a working definition of "belonging to a community of believers" so that we are all on the same page going in to this week's reading plan.

John Ortberg writes: *"God uses people to form people. That is why what happens between you and another person is never merely human to human interaction-the Spirit longs to be powerfully at work in every encounter."*

Here, we learn that the purpose for community living is to ensure we have environments where Spirit-driven, life-giving experiences can flourish.

Solomon went into a courtroom to watch a trial, and witnessed innocent people being oppressed. The poor and powerless began to weep, but no one was there to hear their weeping and no one was there to bring them comfort. It is as if these people had no one to do life with. Where were the worshipers of God? People were experiencing trauma and no one was there to bear their burden.

I used to pray that God would put hurting people in my life, but then I realized that hurting people are everywhere. We don't have to pray that God will put hurting people in our paths; all we need to do is open up our eyes to the oppressed that are all around us. This should be our prayer: "God, get our noses out of our narcissistic affairs and open our blind eyes to the hurting all around."

Solomon draws us to all of the heartache, pain, and calamity that we will experience and says, "You're going to need other people to do life with." You have two options: 1) Will you be flying solo when you are going through difficult seasons? Very few, if any, make it out alive when doing life alone. 2) Will you belong to community of people who will care for and encourage you? Solomon suggests the second option.

Ecclesiastes 4:9-12

Two are better than one, because they have a good reward for their toil. For if they fall, one will lift up his fellow. But woe to him who is alone when he falls and has not another to lift him up! Again, if two lie together, they keep warm, but how can one keep warm alone? And though a man might prevail against one who is alone, two will withstand him—a threefold cord is not quickly broken.

Living in Gospel-centered community is a refrain in the Bible that so few take seriously. Yet, the quicker we realize we need each other, the better off we will be in our spiritual journey. When Solomon mentions that "two are better than one" and "a threefold cord is not quickly broken," he is reminding us of the importance of belonging to a tribe of believers.

Solomon points out that when we are involved in a community of believers, we can have better productivity, better results, and greater security. When one traveled, falling into a pit could mean death if a friend was not there to lift you out. In ancient Israel, sleeping alone couldn't keep travelers warm or safe, which is why those on a journey would often lay with their backs against one another at night. Thieves were also common threat in this particular time as people journeyed from one place to another, but those who traveled together could offer a defense against a thief. What an amazing picture of why we need Gospel-centered community.

Think about the productivity, results, and security we could have if we all locked arms together and did serious life with each other. So, here is my question: why do so few of us participate in deep, meaningful, Gospel-centered relationships? Why do most of us *go to* church rather than *belong to* a church? Belong to a church – because your life depends on it.

11

Ecclesiastes 4:4
*Then I saw that all toil and all skill in work come from a man's envy
of his neighbor. This also is vanity and a striving after wind.*

Yesterday, we were left with a challenging question: "Why do
so few of us participate in deep, meaningful, Gospel-centered
relationships?" We have bought into an American cultural
Christianity that says, "go to church" instead of "belong to a
church." For today and tomorrow, I want us to consider why
we choose cheap social media-like relationships over deep,
meaningful relationships.

There are times in my faith when I am discontent with where
God has me, and it is very difficult to rejoice in other people's
successes. On the flip side, there are times in my faith where
I find myself having a "mountain top experience" and I have
no desire to encourage someone who is failing at something.
Let's be honest, there are even occasions where I rejoice at
other's failings. Could it be that I don't want deep, meaningful
community because I am envious, jealous, and proud? I don't
know how to rejoice when other people do not succeed, nor

do I know how to encourage and mourn when others are falling. These wicked tendencies will kill deep, meaningful community and keep us from belonging to a church.

Today, I want to encourage you to search your heart. Is the reason you do not belong to a church and cultivate relationships due to a jealous and proud heart?

Day

12

Ecclesiastes 4:5
The fool folds his hands and eats his own flesh.

No, this is not a reference to *The Walking Dead*. Here's the translation: "The fool is never satisfied, so he just sits and does nothing." Today, we will talk about one of the core reasons why we choose not to belong to a church community of believers.

I once heard a preacher say that laziness is a comfortable, slow path towards self-destruction. The thing with lazy people is they know what belonging to a community looks like, primarily because they are life-sucking individuals who expect everyone to feed them spiritually. Laziness is also, in my opinion, the number one reason why people leave churches. These lazy people expect the pastor to feed them and be at their beck and call, so they end up looking like a 40-year-old going back to their mothers to be fed like infants. (You're welcome for the visual). The only problem with that is the Bible. The pastor and leadership of this church is modeled

31

after Ephesians 4:11 – "[we will] equip YOU for the work of the ministry for building up the body of Christ."

Will we do ministry with you? You bet. Will we love and encourage you? Yes. Will we hurt when you are hurting? Yes. Will we rejoice when you rejoice? Absolutely. That's what I love to do. But please don't get confused. My primary responsibility is to equip you for the work of ministry.

Laziness is a problem in our American Christian culture. It takes time, energy, and effort to walk in vulnerable relationships with other men and women. How many times have we missed getting to "do life" with others simply because we were too lazy? Don't wait for the pastor or the church leadership to get you involved in the community of the church. Get connected and belong to a church!

Ecclesiastes 5:1

Guard your steps when you go to the house of God. To draw near to listen is better than to offer the sacrifice of fools, for they do not know that they are doing evil.

In Ecclesiastes 5, Solomon begins to address how we approach our God: our worship. When Solomon says, "Guard your steps when you go to the house of God," this could mean to pay attention to the direction of your feet. Wherever your feet are taking you, that will reveal what you are pursuing which, in turn, reveals what you are worshiping.

Solomon lays out three forms of worship in this chapter, but before he does, let us get a working definition of *worship*. Worship is not limited to music, nor is it merely something we do on Sunday. Worship is an expression of adoration and should be evident in everything we do. Paul lays it out like this: "I appeal to you therefore, brothers, by the mercies of God, to present your bodies as a living sacrifice, holy and acceptable to God, which is your spiritual worship" (Romans 12:1 ESV). Paul simply implies that how we live our daily lives is the bedrock of worship. Both living a life of adoration and doing what you were called to do are essential to living a life of worship. Charles H. Spurgeon makes it plain for us: "God is to be praised with the voice, and the heart should go therewith in holy exultation."

To go back to Solomon's point, think about every decision and every thing you do today and ask yourself if it is bringing worship to God. Every morning we should wake up and walk towards Jesus and ask Him to direct our paths.

Are you walking in the direction of the things of God? Are you living a life of worship?

Day

14

Ecclesiastes 5:1-3

Guard your steps when you go to the house of God. To draw near to listen is better than to offer the sacrifice of fools, for they do not know that they are doing evil. Be not rash with your mouth, nor let your heart be hasty to utter a word before God, for God is in heaven and you are on earth. Therefore let your words be few.

Today, we come into a corporate worship setting weekly, but we don't offer animals to the Lord because Jesus fulfilled all the sacrifices in His death on the cross. Besides, no one wants PETA to go crazy on them. As priests of God, we offer up spiritual sacrifices to Jesus. In Ecclesiastes 5:1-3, Solomon tackles several forms of our worship: our words, good works, and money.

Before we talk about how we worship with our words, Solomon advises us to take note of something that has become overlooked in our culture. When you begin to worship, you need to LISTEN to what God is saying to you (v. 1b). So, wherever your feet are taking you, listen to the voice of God for direction. We've forgotten about listening for God's voice because, in our culture, we live in a constant state of distraction. When was the last time you took out your ear buds and put your phone down and asked God to speak to you? The same advice goes for listening to others. When was the last time you sat down with someone and did nothing but lend a listening ear? (Without the distractions of your iPhone.)

According to some studies, people will speak on average of 15,000 words per day. That's a lot of TALK and that puts a lot of things in perspective for me. How many of those words are devoted to God? How many of those words are devoted to encouraging people? How many of those words are devoted to proclaiming the Gospel? It's funny how we speak so eloquently when we give a speech or when we are trying to win someone's affections, yet oftentimes, we don't place as much value on the idle words we speak before the Creator of the cosmos.

Are you using your words to tear people down? Do you speak flippantly before God? Our words are worship when they give life and when they are devoted to our Heavenly Father.

15

Ecclesiastes 5:8-9

If you see in a province the oppression of the poor and the violation of justice and righteousness, do not be amazed at the matter, for the high official is watched by a higher, and there are yet higher ones over them. But this is gain for a land in every way: a king committed to cultivated fields.

Solomon has witnessed the oppression of the poor. The poor were not getting a fair trial and the rich were using them for their own personal gain. Solomon was not surprised by these actions and, in fact, he said that these matters should not amaze us.

How do we reconcile this as a follower of Jesus? What do we do with the powerless? Isaiah 1:17 says, "learn to do good; seek justice, correct oppression; bring justice to the fatherless, plead the widow's cause." This is a theme of the Bible for all believers and is an act of worship to God. In fact, Paul implores us in Colossians 3:17, "And whatever you do, in word or deed, do everything in the name of the Lord Jesus, giving thanks to God the Father through him."

As believers, we have an obligation to stand for the oppressed, poor, least, and last. How many times have we gone through our "province" and witnessed the oppression of the poor and violation of justice and righteousness and have done nothing about it? Our worship is meaningless when we put our hands in our pockets and walk by as if nothing is happening. However, our worship becomes meaningful when we storm the gates of hell on behalf of the powerless.

What can you do to help the powerless?

Ecclesiastes 5:10-12
He who loves money will not be satisfied with money, nor he who loves wealth with his income; this also is vanity. When goods increase, they increase who eat them, and what advantage has their owner but to see them with his eyes? Sweet is the sleep of a laborer, whether he eats little or much, but the full stomach of the rich will not let him sleep.

Solomon has already taught us about the futility of wealth, but now he addresses several myths we believe when it comes to our wealth (or lack thereof). Most people, especially those with financial struggles, will believe one of these lies when it comes to money – that money will bring satisfaction (V. 10), that money will solve every problem (V. 11), or that money will bring peace and security (V. 12). We've already mentioned this, but Solomon had more wealth than anyone could ever imagine, so it would be good for our soul if we listen to his instructions.

Money is one of those topics that people get nervous about, partly because it reveals the direction of their feet. Remember that in verse 1? Watch the direction of your feet, or watch the direction of your spending, because it will reveal what you are worshiping. Jesus said in Matthew 6:21, "For where your treasure is, there your heart will be also." In other words, whatever you value and whatever you're spending all of your money on will determine the essence of your heart, affections, and discipline. Furthermore, that will determine your worldview. So, if your affections are on earthly things, then your mind will justify a life that focuses on the temporal.

Do you know how I know this is true? Because we can justify buying new clothes or a new car, but we have a hard time giving a single dollar to a kid in poverty, or we have an even more difficult time giving to our local church.

How can you shift your view of money to be less focused on yourself and more focused on the kingdom of God?

Ecclesiastes 5:19-20

Everyone also to whom God has given wealth and possessions and power to enjoy them, and to accept his lot and rejoice in his toil—this is the gift of God. For he will not much remember the days of his life because God keeps him occupied with joy in his heart.

Solomon has made the case that our worship is more than mere music echoing in the church halls; rather, it is a life where we worship with our words, actions, and finances. When we reach our final day on earth and we are able to look back on a life of contentment in what God has given us, our hearts will be filled with joy. But this only comes from a worshipful heart. If we live our life full of worry and selfishness, then our expiration date will be marked with sorrow. When we accept God's gift for us today, there will be meaningful enjoyment of the present.

The final verses of this chapter call for every believer to worship God and accept and enjoy the blessings He has given us. The heart only finds satisfaction when we focus on the eternal and tune our hearts to the rhythmic melodies of Heaven.

What are some ways you can use your words, actions, and finances to bring glory to God?

Ecclesiastes 6:1-2

There is an evil that I have seen under the sun, and it lies heavy on mankind: a man to whom God gives wealth, possessions, and honor, so that he lacks nothing of all that he desires, yet God does not give him power to enjoy them, but a stranger enjoys them. This is vanity; it is a grievous evil.

The ability to enjoy life is a God-given gift and cannot be found in anything under the sun. In Ecclesiastes 6, Solomon addresses our discontentment due to seeking satisfaction apart from God. We become discontent when we pursue more and more without looking to God for fulfillment. Whether we realize it or not, our culture is telling us that what we currently have is not good enough, so we need the latest and sexiest thing. Sadly, we buy in to this lie and find ourselves running on the treadmill of discontentment, never finding true joy or fulfillment.

Our culture has launched a marketing campaign that tells that you should be skinny and stylish, that your relationships should be effortless, that you should be having the best sex of your life, that you need the latest toys and trinkets--- and on and on I could go. The reason why I know the majority of us live discontented lives is because we believe these lies. And please don't get me started with social media. We're always comparing our lives to the edited, digital lives of our peers and friends, wondering if we're missing out on something. So how do we handle this? We try to outdo other people by spending more and living pretentious lives.

The key to living a life of contentment lies in enjoying how God has wired us and enjoying the gifts He has given us. Paul said in Philippians 4:11, "I have learned, in whatever state I am, to be content."

Instead of wanting more and comparing your life to your peers and friends, how can you begin to live a life of contentment?

Ecclesiastes 6:1-6

There is an evil that I have seen under the sun, and it lies heavy on mankind: a man to whom God gives wealth, possessions, and honor, so that he lacks nothing of all that he desires, yet God does not give him power to enjoy them, but a stranger enjoys them. This is vanity; it is a grievous evil. If a man fathers a hundred children and lives many years, so that the days of his years are many, but his soul is not satisfied with life's good things, and he also has no burial, I say that a stillborn child is better off than he. For it comes in vanity and goes in darkness, and in darkness its name is covered. Moreover, it has not seen the sun or known anything, yet it finds rest rather than he. Even though he should live a thousand years twice over, yet enjoy no good—do not all go to the one place?

Solomon has identified three areas where discontentment can be found, the first of which is in our wealth and possessions. He references someone who has a great deal of wealth, yet has the ability to enjoy it. I think this happens to most of us because we are stuck in the never-ending cycle of materialism. One of the dark parts of this passage is that Solomon says that no matter how much you possess, if you don't possess the power to enjoy it, you might as well never have been born (v. 3).

Idolatry, the sin of elevating anything above God, is one of the issues that is birthed from discontentment. In this case, we are tempted to enjoy the gifts of God over the Gift-Giver (God Himself). And that is why we are stuck in this cycle. We will never have the ability to enjoy the gifts of God until we learn to be content with what He has given us today.

Solomon's message of how to find contentment has been lost on our culture today, but we can heed his advice. Enjoy the blessings of God today. Be content with how God has wired you. Stop focusing on what you don't have and focus on how you can use what you do have to build the kingdom of God.

How can you use your current wealth and possessions to further the kingdom of God today?

Day
20

Ecclesiastes 6:7-9

All the toil of man is for his mouth, yet his appetite is not satisfied. For what advantage has the wise man over the fool? And what does the poor man have who knows how to conduct himself before the living? Better is the sight of the eyes than the wandering of the appetite: this also is vanity and a striving after wind.

Have you ever wondered why you have to get a job? When I was a teenager my father made all of his children go to work. Unlike most typical teenagers, I didn't mind getting a real job and I learned the valuable lesson of what it means to be responsible. This is a value that I still have and will pass on to my children. I have also found that the reason why most of us work so hard is to pay our bills, buy more things, and fill our refrigerators. However, no matter how hard we work, the bills will keep coming, our clothes will fade, and our refrigerators will get empty. In fact, no matter how rich or how poor you are, you will get hungry again within 8-10 hours of eating (2-3 hours for us Americans).

Solomon is not suggesting that any of us quit our jobs and live in the woods. Instead, he is bringing awareness to the danger of never being content with our thirst to satisfy our worldly cravings. Is it wrong to eat? No. We need food in order to keep our bodies moving. But what good is moving if I'm not moving in the right direction? Solomon would simply tell us that if life is only about working and eating, then our appetites are controlling us, and that is extremely dangerous.

In the end, there can be much enjoyment in working and eating, but we must labor for God's kingdom and enjoy the gifts God has given us without keeping Him out of the picture.

Day

21

Ecclesiastes 6:10-12

Whatever has come to be has already been named, and it is known what man is, and that he is not able to dispute with one stronger than he. The more words, the more vanity, and what is the advantage to man? For who knows what is good for man while he lives the few days of his vain life, which he passes like a shadow? For who can tell man what will be after him under the sun?

Every child goes through the annoying phase of asking the never-ending question: "Why?"

My children were no exception. In fact, they are still going through it. For them, there is never a resolution to life's most pressing questions. For example: Child: "Why is the grass green?" Me: "Because grass produces a bright pigment called chlorophyll. Chlorophyll mostly reflects green light." Child: "Why?" Me: "Well, because I also fertilize it and I have an unusual obsession with grass." Child: "Why?" "Because I like green lush grass." Child: "Why?" Me: Because I have an old man's soul?" Child: "Why?" Me: "Because my father and grandfather made me cut the grass as a young child." Child: "Why?" Me: Walks away in frustration…

It seems that some of us never grow out of this phase. We want to know answers to some of life's most pressing questions and we get frustrated when we hit dead ends, but Solomon tells us that it is meaningless to question the Creator of the cosmos. It simply doesn't do any good to argue with God. Continuously asking God "why" will lead to more questions and more frustrations. Instead, our lack of answers should lead us to a deeper faith in God.

Getting an answer for life's questions doesn't always give peace in your soul. Do the results of an X-ray bring healing? An answer may provide clarity, but it doesn't provide healing. What God knows and what He wills is ultimately for our good, because He knows more about who we are and the situations we are in than we do.

I don't think it's necessarily a bad thing to ask questions, but ultimately if we get caught up in the questions, we could possibly miss the valuable lessons that God is trying to teach us. God does not feel threatened when we question Him, but it is important to love Him and trust the plan that He has for us.

Hold up there, Kemosabe

The previous chapters have been largely focused on areas of our lives in which we find discontentment. Solomon has shared that most of us are discontent with our possessions, wealth, work, and the unknown. But how do we reconcile that with living in a world that teaches us to live a life for the temporal? Furthermore, how do we live a life where we can thoroughly enjoy all of the gifts God has given us?

The first thing we can do is live in the present. The ability to live in the now comes from within, yet it is a hard thing to do with all of the world's distractions. Learning to lean in to the present and witnessing the movement of God *now* is a sure way to find contentment. However, many of us are so focused on the future that we miss out on what God is doing now. God is moving in our families, our situations, our communities, and our churches, but most of us will miss it because we are so focused on what's happening tomorrow or next week.

The second thing we can do is look to Jesus and allow Him to be in complete control. It is through Him that we will find our contentment. The discontentment of our hearts reveals that we aren't allowing Jesus to be in complete control. When we look to Jesus, we will see that we are free from the burdens of this world. We now have the ability to see that we are forgiven, we are counted as righteous, and He gives us peace, purpose, significance, and the opportunity to enjoy life.

"Keep your life free from love of money, and be content with what you have, for he has said, 'I will never leave you nor forsake you.' So we can confidently say, 'The Lord is my helper; I will not fear; what can man do to me?'" Hebrews 13:5-6

The remedy to the love of money, possessions, and knowledge, is contentment, which comes only when we trust in God's sovereignty. When we realize that God is the source of our satisfaction and He is in complete control, then we will step into a rushing surge of peace and contentment.

This means that I have to give up control, which is extremely difficult for me to do as a leader. When I am struggling, I have to trust that God, in His sovereignty, is going to take care of what I'm going through. He loves us too much to leave us and forsake us. This also means that I need to learn to be grateful for what I have instead of always wanting what is new and different.

Has the love of "new" and "different" created a barrier in your relationship with God?

How can you quench the temptation for more in order for you to live in and enjoy your present life? Have you fully surrendered your life to Jesus?

22

Ecclesiastes 7:1a
A good name is better than precious ointment [...].

For the past six chapters, Solomon has taken us on a "meaningless" adventure ride. He's told us that he is better than we are, more powerful than we will ever be, more wealthy than we will ever be, and has more experience with pleasure than we will ever have. Yet, in the end, he has found that it is meaningless. Chapter 7 moves us away from his experience and in to an impartation of wisdom. In fact, if your bible contains section headings, this chapter may read "The Contrast of Wisdom and Folly."

The words *name* and *ointment* (v. 1) are most likely plays on words. In the Hebrew, *name* translates to *sheem* while *ointment* translates to *shemen*. Since ointment was a costly luxury, one could assume that Solomon is talking about how we spend so much money and time trying to make ourselves look good externally, while the growth of our character is left undeveloped. We can go to the gym, get Botox and tummy tucks, apply anti-cellulite creams, eat greens and drink cleansers; but at the end of your life, who cares how you look if your personality and character stinks?

The desire for external rather than internal beauty has become a cancer to our culture, but this is only the outworking of our discontentment. We are wrong when we convince ourselves that our name is only as good as our appearance, and we strive in vain to find peace in the external. We have tried to live in an idealistic world where everything appears "put together," so we end up looking good on the outside but smelling like a rotten corpse on the inside. This form of demonic "Christianity" focuses only on the external, while God is interested in the heart.

Our devotion to appearance rather than growing in character is similar to a grown man swimming in the kiddie pool--- onlookers question it because the two do not seem to go together. Likewise, real character does not develop as our appearances become more pleasing. Do you know what freaks me out? Seeing a grown man with no kids swimming in the kiddie pool. This should cause concern for everyone.

In the end, what God is after is our heart, not the external. If we surrender our heart to Jesus, then the rest will take care of itself.

Why do we pretend that our lives are "put together" while our hearts are in despair? How have you given more concern to how you are viewed than the growth of your soul and character?

Day

23

Ecclesiastes 7:1-2

A good name is better than precious ointment, and the day of death than the day of birth. It is better to go to the house of mourning than to go to the house of feasting, for this is the end of all mankind, and the living will lay it to heart.

It would seem that Solomon has lost his mind. Seriously? Death is better than birth? I remember when my children were born and it was an amazing moment in my life. I remember vividly how it impacted me. It seemed as if all of the earth stood still and I wept with both joy and slight fear. I have since started to have dreams and aspirations for them. I don't want them to live in my shadow; rather, I dream that they will live their lives to the fullest and do what God has purposed them to do. I want to walk my baby girl down the aisle and watch my boys marry the girls of their dreams. Yet, wouldn't it be a tragedy if I died before any of that happened? Not according to Solomon. Solomon is pointing out that death for every believer is not the end but the beginning.

I believe it is crucial for us to consider death. The realization of our own mortality will cause a lot of introspection. I don't tend to contemplate the state of my soul or my relationship with God when I'm at a party or when life is going well, but find me at a funeral and I will be doing a lot of soul examination.

In my time of introspection, I have begun to find that things do not matter. I know that sounds like a churchy cliché, but it's true. In fact, I long for the day when I'm not worried about my image. My earnest prayer is that I will live a life fully abandoned to Christ. I want to be known by God and live an abundant life for His kingdom. I want to be more generous. I don't want to be famous or build an empire. I just want Jesus. Yet, it's not just that I *want* Jesus; He is my only option. I want to echo what Paul said in Philippians 3:10: "I want to know Christ and the power of his resurrection, and that I may share his sufferings, becoming like him in his death, that by any means possible I may attain the resurrection from the dead."

Although introspection can be painful, I would highly recommend it. The Bible reiterates the importance of concerning ourselves with our hearts and not our reputations because all that matters in the end is the posture of our hearts, not how good we look.

Are you more concerned with how you appear externally than internally?

Ecclesiastes 7:5
It is better for a man to hear the rebuke of the wise than to hear the song of fools.

Can I tell you something that I really hate hearing? Rebuke. When someone rebukes me, the first thing I want to do is counter that rebuke with more rebuke. "Oh, I have sin? Well, Kemosabe, you've had a stinky attitude as of late, and your breath smells like a goat." Maybe I've admitted too much? Let's move on, then.

Generally, rebuke should come when we are doing something that is out of step with the Bible or perhaps out of step with our character. Rebuke should also, most of the time, come from people you trust. Receiving rebuke is never fun, but it is essential to our spiritual development. As Solomon says in Proverbs 27:17, "Iron sharpens iron, and one man sharpens another." This is not just a cute verse fit for a coffee cup; rather, it is an extremely painful process.

How much energy would we save if we were just honest about our issues and allowed people to engage our hearts? People who are wise will not be afraid to have people engage their hearts and point out the wrongs they are doing. However, the fool welcomes people who encourage his foolish behavior.

Are you the wise person who allows rebuke in your life to help you grow spiritually? Or are you the foolish one who only listens to people who will encourage your messy lifestyle?

Day

25

Ecclesiastes 7:6
For as the crackling of thorns under a pot, so is the laughter of the fools; this also is vanity.

There have been seasons in my life where I found myself going through a funk. The kind of funk where I'm cranky, I don't want to be around anyone, and I feel like my soul is on fire. I know it's hard to believe, but I was a Negative Nelly and just couldn't see any good in anything. After spending time with a group of men and my counselor one week, I felt like I was getting better. Later in the week, though, a friend of mine came by my house and asked me how I was doing and, of course, I gave him the Christian response: "I'm great, man." Then came the gentle rebuke: "Seriously, Matthew? Let's cut to the chase and tell me how you're really doing!"

I should probably confess that my wife had to contact some of my friends to come and check on me, so honestly, if it wasn't for her, I'd probably still be in a funk today because of my stubbornness. In all seriousness, though, I needed to be honest with those around me. I ended up learning that the concern and prayer of others was cool water thrown on the fire that was raging in my soul.

I find Ecclesiastes 7:6 so intriguing because Solomon is talking about me. It's as if the fire of trauma is consuming us and, all the while, we laugh as if everything is okay! What? So your soul is burning and it's no big deal?

It is the wise man who screams for help. Instead of living in denial, he admits that he is suffering, that he has a heart issue, and that he is deteriorating on the inside, and he screams for help.

The amazing thing about the Gospel is that Jesus came for the burn victims. We don't have to pretend that we aren't on fire. We can come to a place and say, "No, I'm not okay. My soul and world is engulfed in flames." And the amazing thing is that Jesus will not push us away; rather, He will draw us in to His ocean of grace to put out the fires in our soul.

It is vital that our churches continue to be a hospital for the burn victims. However, in order for us to do that, we too must admit that we are burn victims. God delights in our burns and he is not afraid to engage them and put them out.

Are you pretending to be "okay," while inwardly you are screaming for help? Jesus says, "Come." He is the doctor who will heal the hurts of your heart.

Ecclesiastes 7:7-10

Surely oppression drives the wise into madness, and a bribe corrupts the heart. Better is the end of a thing than it's beginning, and the patient in spirit is better than the proud in spirit. Be not quick in your spirit to become angry, for anger lodges in the heart of fools. Say not, "Why were the former days better than these?" For it is not from wisdom that you ask this.

The moment when you surrender your life to Jesus you have a new "end goal". The end goal for every regenerate believer changes from self-serving to ushering the Kingdom of God in our surroundings. So, as parents, our end goal is not to raise celebrity athletes or moral people, but rather to impart Jesus to them and pray the Gospel takes deep root in their souls. As married couples, our end goal is not to have the best sex of our lives. As husbands, our end goal is to love our wives as Christ loved the church. My wife is not to have some super macho man who will drive her wild at night; rather, she is to submit to my sacrificial, tender-loving leadership. So when we talk about end goals, things can get complicated and it's important that everyone is on the same page. Our end goal is Jesus and submitting to the commands He has given us.

It's also important for me to be constantly reminded of the end goal of the church I planted. It's incredible to be a part of Refuge Point, a multi-cultural and multi-generational church. When my wife and I planted Refuge Point, I never wanted a young, "white church." I have always said that if that were the case, I would have just joined another "white church" in our area. Our end goal for Refuge Point is to reflect Revelation 7:9-10 which says, *"I saw a great multitude of every race of people crying out 'Salvation belongs to the Jesus"* (paraphrase). Imagine a church that is tearing down the walls of racial hostility and is a reflection of Heaven!

When we aren't seeing the results we expect, sometimes we can be tempted to respond, "The good old days were better than this." We end up idolizing the past, and conveniently ignoring the positives around us. One of the expectations that people had when we first planted Refuge Point was that we would do church the way it "used to be." We would respond by lovingly pointing them to our belief that God wanted to do a new thing, and that those who attended should expect church to look a lot different than the past. It reminds me of when the second temple was being built in Ezra 3. The young men sang songs of rejoicing and the old men wept for "the good old days." Let us be reminded of what God wants to do in our lives. Haggai called out the promise of the Lord when the people were lamenting about the former days: "The latter glory of this house shall be greater than the former, says the LORD of hosts. And in this place I will give peace, declares the LORD of hosts." (Haggai 2:9)

Ephesians 3:20 says, "Now to him who is able to do far more abundantly than all that we ask or think, according to the power at work within us." God can do more than you ask or think, and it will be better than anything that has taken place in your past. ***Praise Break*** No matter your age or race, God is able to do more than you can imagine. Why do we cling to our past when God has a far better plan for our future?

How should your way of living change with the "end goal" in mind?

Day
27

Ecclesiastes 7:14-15

In the day of prosperity be joyful, and in the day of adversity consider: God has made the one as well as the other, so that man may not find out anything that will be after him. In my vain life I have seen everything. There is a righteous man who perishes in his righteousness, and there is a wicked man who prolongs his life in his evildoing.

Solomon's tone has almost turned sarcastic in nature. Here, he says that life is going to be good at times and tough at times, so just remain calm. No matter how hard you try, you can't control most of it. Interestingly enough, life doesn't fit into a neat pattern of punishment and rewards.

It reminds me of a game I play with my son. When he tries to start a fight with me, I always tell him, "If you mess with fire; you will get burned." Low and behold, he plays with fire and I burn him. We all believe this in some way. In fact, Eastern Mysticism calls this concept "Karma:" whatever you do, good or bad, you will get what you deserve.

This is what all religions believe, including some Christians. If you did something bad and received your punishment, you got what you deserved. If you were a bad boy and momma whooped you, you got what you deserved. If you worked hard and received a raise, you got what you deserved. If you do good, then the universe will align itself correctly and give you what you deserve. If you are bad, then Karma will "come back and bite you."

However, Solomon disagrees. He says, "I've seen wise great men perish and I've seen evil men prosper." Why do bad things happen to good people? Why do the innocent suffer? Why did 9/11 happen? Why are Coptic Christians being persecuted in Egypt today?

The Gospel counters the idea of "getting what you deserve." Indeed, you deserve death, but Jesus, who knew no sin, became sin so that we wouldn't get what we deserve (II Cor. 5:21). God has flipped the bill and has given us grace.

How can your understanding of God's grace help you to treat others who have done wrong?

28

Ecclesiastes 7:16

Be not overly righteous, and do not make yourself too wise. Why should you destroy yourself?

That sounds awesome, right? Don't be overly righteous? I think we have all nailed that down pretty well. Oh, wait – he's actually talking about something else. Solomon is actually warning against *self*-righteousness. Self-righteousness is when I have a small view of my own sin and have a bigger view of others' sin. Basically I think I'm a good person mainly because I'm not doing any "major" sinning.

While various sins may lead to various earthly consequences, in light of eternity, all sin is the same. We may stretch the truth, but at least we aren't killing anyone. At least we behave most of the time, are mostly morally upright people, and we aren't like the terrible people in this world. We're okay! Right? Actually, no, we're not.

What we are doing, in essence, is basing our salvation on our good deeds. However, if our good deeds can make us right before God, then the work of the cross was in vain. This is the culture of do-good-ism, which says, "If I just do good things, then God will be pleased with me." However, Solomon warns that doing good works and being self-righteous will end up destroying you.

Isaiah 64:6 says, "We have all become like one who is unclean, and all our righteous deeds are like a polluted garment." The Bible just said that even if we are morally batting at 1000, we are a stench before God. Our salvation is based on what Christ has already done for us, not anything we can do. We must realize that we don't have to come to God all cleaned up. God loves who we are right now, not who we think we ought to be.

Have you placed your trust in your good works or in the work of Christ on the cross?

29

Ecclesiastes 7:23

All this I have tested by wisdom. I said, "I will be wise," but it was far from me. That which has been is far off, and deep, very deep; who can find it out?

At this point, Solomon has tried to be good and wise apart from God and found he could not do it. Since no one can be right and wise and since foolishness leads to death, what are we to do? Is there any hope for us? Or are we doomed to get what we deserve?

This is what I love about the Gospel and what sets it apart from every other religion. In the middle of us trying to gain understanding, trying to be good and bad, and in the middle of us getting what we deserve, God steps in and gives us the grace we don't deserve. Mormons rely on works, Jehovah's Witnesses rely on works, Muslims rely on works, Buddhists rely on works, and on and on I could go, but that is not what Jesus is about. In the middle of us deserving the penalty of death, Jesus absorbed all of my do-good-ism, sin, and shame and wiped it clean. He then counts me as righteous, not because of anything I did or could do, but by His saving work on the cross.

This is why I am grateful that God loves me for who I am now and not some future version of myself. God is not waiting for me to get my junk together or for me to conquer every sin in my life in order for Him to rain His grace down. He is even pleased with me in my struggling, stumbling, and confusion.

It's as if my life is a piece of music that God is composing. He writes one measure at a time and can already hear the next, while I am clearly deaf to the unwritten measures. How shocking is it to know that God loves us now? He loves our current measure of this musical masterpiece that He is composing. For me, it's hard to understand, but it's where I find rest and comfort.

How can this realization change the way we view ourselves and those around us?

Ecclesiastes 7:26-29

And I find something more bitter than death: the woman whose heart is snares and nets, and whose hands are fetters. He who pleases God escapes her, but the sinner is taken by her. Behold, this is what I found, says the Preacher, while adding one thing to another to find the scheme of things—which my soul has sought repeatedly, but I have not found. One man among a thousand I found, but a woman among all these I have not found. See, this alone I found, that God made man upright, but they have sought out many schemes.

Houston, we have a problem. And it's not with women! Solomon had partied more than anyone could ever party and had built more than Donald Trump could build. He moved from the party scene to the women scene. Yes, I said *women,* not *woman.* He started with trying to find a mythical creature (i.e. a woman who will fill all of the emptiness in his heart.) The problem was that the first wife didn't work, so he married wife number two. Shockingly, he eventually had 700 wives and 300 concubines.

I'm going to go on a limb here and suggest that the problem wasn't the women; rather, the problem lay within Solomon.

Our boy Solomon had a sexual issue. Solomon viewed women as merely a tool to fulfill his sexual needs. Furthermore, in Solomon's efforts to fulfill his desires, he got caught up with some women who enticed him away from the Lord and into the worship of idols.

Sadly, the search for "the one" and the search to have our sexual fantasies met continues today for both men and women, and it leads to destruction. Although we may not have 700 spouses and 300 hookers at our side, our problems today may be in the form of pornography or sex with multiple partners.

Let's all collectively agree that, like Solomon, our view of sex and marriage is broken. Every Sunday, there are men and women sitting in our churches who are struggling with an addiction to pornography. There are men and women in our churches who are having sex with multiple people. What about the married men and women in our churches who are flirting with someone who isn't their spouse, or even having affairs? We find ourselves in the same predicament as Solomon – we are trying to fill the emptiness in our hearts that only Jesus can fill. Even though this issue is extremely commonplace, most churches remain silent.

Instead of focusing our time and energy on finding "the one," God wants us to find contentment in Him. He desires to make us more like Him so that we can be a better "one" for our future spouse. There is not a man or woman that can make you feel complete. Only Jesus possesses the power to make us whole.

How do you view relationships, marriage, and sex? Have you tried seeking contentment in God?

31

Ecclesiastes 8:1

Who is like the wise? And who knows the interpretation of a thing?
A man's wisdom makes his face shine, and the hardness of his face
is changed.

Before we get into some interesting topics in this chapter,
Solomon wants to make a crucial statement that should be
a reality for every believer. When he talks about a "face
that shines," it is important to know that this only comes
when we are in communion with God. Because we live in a
post-New Testament world, we now have the light of Christ
in our hearts (2 Corinthians 4:6). This is incredible news!
Whatever obstacle we encounter in life, whether it be in our
jobs, schools, families, communities, or government, we have
a power source that can push out the darkness and help us
overcome.

However, this should not create an "us vs. them" mentality.
We aren't the holier than thou's who fight against the terrible
sinners in the world. On the contrary, what this means is
that the light that pours from our hearts is radiating God's

grace and love to those who are in darkness. It is not a call for Christians to shake our fists and point our fingers in the face of our culture. For far too long, the church has been known for what we are against rather than what we are for. We should engage our dark culture with the light of Christ, radiating His love and grace.

Furthermore, we don't have to be like little children who are scared of the dark. We have a light that is powerful enough to push out the darkness in our jobs, families, communities, and nation. How do we do this? Solomon will address it in the next few verses (sorry for the cliffhanger).

Day

32

Ecclesiastes 8:2-4

I say: Keep the king's command, because of God's oath to him. Be not hasty to go from his presence. Do not take your stand in an evil cause, for he does whatever he pleases. For the word of the king is supreme, and who may say to him, "What are you doing?"

We can all agree that we live in a broken world. There are broken churches, families, institutions, and governments. These things are broken because the people within them are broken. In the midst of the brokenness, it is important to be careful whom you are submitting to. In the end, you could end up in an awful situation.

One of the reasons why we need to be careful to whom we submit to is because we are called to respect their authority (v. 2). I'm not saying that you have to agree with them, but you do have to submit to their leadership. Consider our former President, Obama. This is a man who is highly disrespected by the majority of the Christian community. For too long I have seen Christian people belittle this man, when the Bible has called us to pray for him. I resolved in my heart that

I could never change his mind on many issues on which I disagreed with him, but I could pray that God could change his heart. Seriously, do you think that God was surprised that he was elected the President of the USA? Maybe we ought to exchange our social media rants with fervent prayer for the president. Maybe you have a boss who is a complete JERK or maybe it's your spouse or parents – you are called to pray for those in authority.

So, what happens when we are in an abusive situation or the authority in our lives is pushing us to do something that is outside of what the Bible teaches? Wait for it… here's another cliffhanger. Solomon will address this in verse 3 (tomorrow's reading). Side Note: If you are in an abusive relationship, get out and get help! I wouldn't want to be on the receiving end of the abuse, nor would I expect anyone else to receive the abuse.

Ecclesiastes 8:3-4

Be not hasty to go from his presence. Do not take your stand in an evil cause, for he does whatever he pleases. For the word of the king is supreme, and who may say to him, "What are you doing?"

Yesterday, we asked what we, as Christians, are to do if we are in an abusive situation or if an authority figure expects us to do something that is outside of what the Bible teaches. Our boy Solomon gives us a pretty clear answer found in verse 3, which echoes many other passages in the Bible – we stay defiant. We are not to give in to the wickedness that surrounds us. The Apostle Peter says it best in Acts 5:29: "Obey God rather than men." Now, this doesn't mean that we resist the law on every matter, but it means that we can't do anything that is counter to the word of God.

Consider the late and great Dr. Martin Luther King, Jr. With the light of Christ burning in his soul, MLK marched in the face of adversity and pushed out what was dark. What about today? Who are the MLK's of our generation? Who will stand in the face of evil and be a voice to the 59 million aborted babies? Who will be a voice for the 5 million Syrian refugees, half of which are children? Who will stand up for the 400,000 foster children in America? Who will stand against the gangs who usher drugs and violence into our communities? Who will stand against the abused? Who will stand against those in power who oppress the poor or cause believers to do something that is counter to their faith?

Christians don't want to answer these questions because it requires us to come out of our comfort zones. We want to live comfortably while expecting someone else to defy evil on our behalf. We are worried about our next pair of shoes, how big our next house should be, what type of outfit we need, what sport our kids should play – and we stay silent about what really matters. What we are doing is defying God and saying we don't care about the commands He has given us. Meanwhile, there are hurting people all around us.

Where evil resides, it is our obligation to stand up, defy it, and shine the light of Christ. Solomon also wrote in Proverbs 31:8-9, "Open your mouth for the mute, for the rights of all who are destitute. Open your mouth, judge righteously, defend the rights of the poor and needy." Also, Isaiah 1:17 says, "Learn to do good; seek justice, correct oppression; bring justice to the fatherless, plead the widow's cause." These are but a few verses throughout the Bible that charge all Jesus-followers to be defiant against evil.

What will you do in the face of evil? The world needs no more silent and lazy Christians. With the light of Christ burning in our hearts, I know the darkness can be defeated.

Day

33

Ecclesiastes 8:5

"Whoever keeps a command will know no evil thing, and the wise heart will know the proper time and the just way. For there is a time and a way for everything, although man's trouble lies heavy on him."

It is difficult to rise up against any injustice or evil authority in this world, but the Bible charges us to be a light in the darkness and not waiver in our faith. However, I would like to give you a few points to consider before you go to war with culture:

USE GENTLENESS AND WISDOM

Maybe picketing isn't a good idea after all. Peaceful protest is an American right, but you may end up alienating more people than you convince. Pointing your finger in people's faces never has accomplished anything, but what if we used wisdom and tried to engage the oppressors? Stay with me for a minute and consider Daniel in the Old Testament. A prisoner of war in a Gentile land, Daniel refused to eat the unclean food, but he didn't make a huge scene about it. He didn't boycott McDonalds, nor did picket Starbucks. He used gentleness and wisdom, so he suggested a different diet. The plan worked and in the end, his gentle wisdom led to a promotion (Daniel 1).

USE DISCERNMENT

Clearly, we have not mastered the art of discernment. We are more like the fool who storms off, overreacts, and starts cleaning out our guns. Using discernment means we are acting synonymously with Jesus. It means that we are slow to speak. 1 Thessalonians 5:21-22 teaches us to "test everything…" In other words, using discernment is the ability to measure all things with the word of God. So before we riot in the streets ask yourself; "what is the Lord telling us?" "What does the word of God tell us to do?" Rioting maybe called for. Being a screaming prophet may be appropriate. But use judgement. Don't get yourself killed over Disney World having a celebration week for something you don't agree with.

THERE WILL BE REPERCUSSIONS

For some reason, American Christians are shocked when there is persecution. The Apostles weren't shocked. These men and women were beaten, arrested, and imprisoned; however, they showed respect to their authorities and were willing to suffer for their faith. Do not be shocked when you are persecuted for standing in the face of evil.

Until Jesus sets up his righteous kingdom, there will always be injustice in our world. So what do we do? We use discernment and wisdom, we fight, we are defiant, we vote, and we labor.

Day
34

Ecclesiastes 8:15
And I commend joy, for man has nothing better under the sun but to eat and drink and be joyful, for this will go with him in his toil through the days of his life that God has given him under the sun.

It is critical that we examine this verse with a careful eye, because Solomon is not suggesting that we subscribe to the "eat, drink, and be merry" philosophy. This is not a call for self-indulgence. Rather, Solomon is suggesting that we accept and enjoy all God has given us. Instead of complaining about our situations or what we don't have, we rejoice in what we do have.

Solomon is suggesting that we live our life to the fullest while being content with what God has given us. How do we live life to the fullest? We do so by being fully present. It's extremely difficult to do this in our culture. There are millions of distractions vying for our attention, making it difficult to live in the present. How many times have we been in the same room with our spouses or kids yet are not mentally there? If we allow the distractions to dominate our attention, we will miss God's movement in our lives.

How do we live life to the fullest? It starts with us resting. It starts with us being content with what we currently have. It starts with us staying connected to the people we love. It starts with us inviting the least, last, and lost into our lives. It starts with us feasting with our family and friends. No matter what life throws at you, this is how we are to live.

Day

35

Ecclesiastes 9:1-3

But all this I laid to heart, examining it all, how the righteous and the wise and their deeds are in the hand of God. Whether it is love or hate, man does not know; both are before him. It is the same for all, since the same event happens to the righteous and the wicked, to the good and the evil, to the clean and the unclean, to him who sacrifices and him who does not sacrifice. As the good one is, so is the sinner, and he who swears is as he who shuns an oath. This is an evil in all that is done under the sun, that the same event happens to all. Also, the hearts of the children of man are full of evil, and madness is in their hearts while they live, and after that they go to the dead.

You've probably noticed by now that Solomon is not a guy who you'd invite over for dinner, especially if you were planning on having a lighthearted evening. In verses 1-3 of Chapter 9, Solomon claims that no matter how you live your life, you don't get to determine the outcome. No matter how righteous or wicked you are, death comes to everyone. Sadly, you don't know when that's going to happen. No matter how much you work out or stuff yourself with greens, death is going to get you eventually (Depressed? Keep reading).

This text doesn't mean that we live passively with no concerns, rather that we are to live our lives today. So, if death is coming for all of us, what are we going to do with the life that we are living? What are you doing that is furthering the Kingdom of God? What are you doing to cultivate the relationships? I have found that the reality of my own death draws me closer to Jesus and my family. Maybe contemplating death isn't a bad idea after all.

Ecclesiastes 9:7
Go, eat your bread with joy, and drink your wine with a merry heart, for God has already approved what you do.

Since this is not a call for self-indulgence or a prosperity message, what does it look like for Christians to enjoy life no matter their circumstances? If you don't believe that a Christian can enjoy life, listen to what John 10:10 says: "The thief comes only to steal and kill and destroy. I came that they may have life and have it abundantly." Wow! Jesus wants us to live life abundantly. What does an abundant life look like?

In order for us to live an abundant life, we must be connected to our *now*. We can't allow our past or our future to rob us of our present. My mind is full of regrets that came with yesterday. I have an issue that causes my mouth to get ahead of my head, also known as foot-in-mouth syndrome. Unfortunately, this also happens on a Sunday while I'm preaching. I understand that some people can't take it, but I will beat myself up for some of the dumb things that have come out of my mouth while preaching. Knowing that some people are critics doesn't help. I also say things to my wife, kids, and people I work with that I regret. This causes me to disconnect from my present because I'm too worried about my past.

If we're always somewhere else, we miss the movement of God in our lives and in those around us. Because we are constantly stuck in our past or looking to the future, we begin operating in broken cycles of thinking. So, how do we enjoy our present life if we are burdened with our past and future? As difficult as it seems, we rest. Sit in awe of God. Slow down. Eat and drink in deeply the richness of His love, grace, and mercy. We can enjoy life when we sit and meditate on Him and when we search for God in everything that is going on.

Is your concern over yesterday or tomorrow keeping you from enjoying your life today?

Ecclesiastes 9:9
Enjoy life with the wife whom you love, all the days of your vain life that he has given you under the sun, because that is your portion in life and in your toil at which you toil under the sun.

Most people believe that Solomon wrote Ecclesiastes later in his life and, if this is true, then this verse reveals that Solomon understands that marrying 700 wives was not a good idea. So, how can we enjoy our spouse if we aren't mentally connected to him or her? In order for you to enjoy your spouse, you have to *be with* your spouse – not just physically, but mentally and spiritually. This lack of connection is one of the most common reasons why marriages end up in trauma.

One of the reasons we can't enjoy our spouses is because our minds are constantly on something or someone else. There are millions of distractions that are vying for our attention at all times. But what would your marriage look like if you stopped fantasizing about someone or something else and spent all of your time cultivating your relationship with your spouse?

I'm sure some of you are thinking, *you don't know my spouse!* Well, actually you don't know your own self. Jeremiah 17:9 says, "The heart is deceitful beyond all things. Who can understand it?" And contrary to what society tells us, the grass isn't greener on the other side. Actually, the grass is greener; you just haven't been there yet to poop on it. Maybe you ought to devote your time to cultivating your own grass instead of fantasizing about someone else's (hopefully, my grass and poop metaphor didn't lose you).

How can you enjoy your spouse? Spend time with your spouse mentally, emotionally, and spiritually. Another way you can enjoy your spouse is by planning special date time. And if you don't know how to date, Google it.

Ecclesiastes 9:7-9

Go, eat your bread with joy, and drink your wine with a merry heart, for God has already approved what you do. Let your garments be always white. Let not oil be lacking on your head. Enjoy life with the wife whom you love, all the days of your vain life that he has given you under the sun, because that is your portion in life and in your toil at which you toil under the sun.

If we are meant to enjoy life by resting and being connected to the present, what happens when we become disconnected? When we get disconnected, we aren't aware of God's presence around us. When we aren't fully present, suddenly life is happening everywhere around us and God's activity always seems to be somewhere else.

There's a story in Genesis 28 where Jacob is in-between a "certain place" and grabs a rock as a pillow. He dreams about the next forty years and wakes up and says, "Surely God has been in this place." The problem is that God had been there all along, but Jacob wasn't aware of it. It wasn't that "God showed up" – no, *Jacob* woke up and showed up. If we are not fully present, then we will miss what God is doing right now and what He has for us. It's always weird when I hear people praying for God to "show up and show out." Fortunately, we don't have to beg God to show up because He is always here. God never leaves us. Rather, we leave Him.

What happens when we're not fully present is the activity of God becomes something that is occurring someplace else. We'll hear about what God is doing in major cities, mega churches, or some major Christian conference and say, "Oh, I want to be a part of that." However, we don't realize that the same God is right here doing major things. Why do you think some people leave one church to go to another church? This is what happens when we aren't obedient to stay where God has placed us. It's time we wake up and realize that God is here *now*. Do not miss God's activity because you are disconnected. Be where you are.

Ecclesiastes 9:7b
...for God has already approved what you do.

Every time I read this verse I want to dance for joy and do a praise break. While I am enjoying all that God has for me and while I am in the process of life, God approves of me. The Hebrew word for *approved* is *Ratsah*, which can also mean "to take pleasure in." So, God is pleased when we find enjoyment in our lives. Furthermore, even when we are going through trauma in our lives, God takes pleasure in us.

This is the insane message of the Gospel – that God takes pleasure in you. Hebrews 13:21 says that [Jesus will] equip you with everything good that you may do his will, working in us that which is pleasing in his sight. So, while God is molding you into His image, he is pleased with you and approves of you as His child. This means that God accepts us while we are in the process of being sanctified, which is a churchy way of saying we are being made more like Jesus each day. God in heaven, the Creator of the cosmos, is pleased with me *now*. Wow. There is no other religion like that.

There are times in my life that I feel inadequate and unqualified and there are times that I have doubts, fears, and feel far from God. Yet, in these times, God approves of me and is pleased with my process. Knowing that God loves us this much should cause us to find rest and enjoyment in whatever season we find ourselves in.

Praise Break!

No really...let's take a second to praise Jesus before we continue with Day 40.

James 1:5-8
If any of you lacks wisdom, let him ask God, who gives generously to all without reproach, and it will be given him.

Have you ever been rejected? I have been rejected many times in my life. In fact, the woman I married once rejected me in high school, but we see she couldn't resist for long. Rejection is never a fun process, especially when people we love are the perpetrators.

The thing I love about this text is that there is no criterion when it comes to asking God for wisdom. He doesn't give a litmus test nor does he expect us to have our act together. He simply says, "If you lack wisdom, ask God, who gives generously to all without reproach." God won't ever reject our request for wisdom.

Ecclesiastes repeatedly covers two commons themes: wisdom and folly. We have read so much about wisdom in this book, but we haven't talked much about foolishness. And we would be foolish not to talk about foolishness. Although the passage above is not taken from Ecclesiastes, it has serious implications for what we are going to go through in the coming days.

Furthermore, this passage reveals that God saved us from our sin – but He didn't save us from our stupidity. That's why He said that we ought to ask for wisdom. And if we live our lives trying to figure out what we can get away with, we are foolish and our thinking pattern needs to change. We have the wonderful privilege of coming to our Father and asking Him to help us avoid stupidity.

Day
40

Ecclesiastes 10:2-3
A wise man's heart inclines him to the right, but a fool's heart to the left. Even when the fool walks on the road, he lacks sense, and he says to everyone that he is a fool.

Solomon is a man who has set out on an adventure to determine the difference between wisdom and foolishness. For most of this book, he talks about how many of us are on the verge of making wrong choices. A lot of us don't seek wisdom; instead, we try to figure out what we can get away with. This will only lead us in making foolish mistakes and, in the end, lead us down a path to destruction. For the next few days, I will discuss some killers of wisdom. Hopefully, learning what obstructs wisdom will help us make wise choices that will keep us on the path of righteousness.

The first killer of wisdom is doubt.

I'm not talking about intellectual doubt. Intellectual doubt is a good thing. It's what keeps me from eating "100% real beef" McDonald's burgers. Really? They're 100% real beef?

I seriously doubt that. Our intellectual doubts have led us to believe that the earth is not flat and that the earth is not the center of the solar system. We need these kinds of doubts to learn and grow.

However, doubting God's goodness, sovereignty, or plan will cause you to make terrible choices. So many times, I think my way of handling a situation is better than God's way. This doubt will cripple me and make me into a fool. I think about the doubts that I had when God called us to plant Refuge Point Church. Seriously, I am the least qualified person to lead a church. Thankfully, I surrendered my doubts and God has written pages of our story that only He could have written. Many lives have been transformed by God's power because we didn't allow doubt to rule us.

Doubt even keeps us from seeing the best in people. Don't believe me? If you text or call me, I may not respond quickly. It's not because I don't like you. It's simply because I'm either working, studying, on the phone, in a meeting, being a husband, being a dad, or on the road. I'm not trying to avoid you either, which is what doubt will make you believe. The doubt in your thinking will always assume the worst about people. As a result, meaningful relationships don't get a chance to form.

In the end, you need to place your trust in God and know that He is good and will never leave or forsake you. Knowing this will keep you on the path of wisdom and away from the folly of doubt.

41

Proverbs 1:7
The fear of the Lord is the beginning of knowledge, but fools despise wisdom and instruction.

For most of this book, Solomon has talked about what he has learned in dealing with foolishness. There are several things that will keep us locked in the prison of foolishness, one of them being fear. You've probably noticed in life that fear and doubt are kissing cousins. The two are almost inseparable. Generally, where there is doubt, fear is lurking around the corner.

Today, you need to decide that whatever you fear establishes the boundaries of your freedom. So, if you fear the dark, then you keep a night-light on. If you fear bugs, then you scream like a girl when one touches you. If you fear the future, then you stay tied to the past. If you fear rejection, then you will spend your whole life defining yourself by others' expectations. Fear establishes boundaries for your freedom and, if you fear God, then you are free. That seems odd, but if you fear God, you walk in knowing that He will care for you and love you, which removes your need to control everything yourself.

This passage from Proverbs, that Solomon also wrote, says the right kind of fear is the beginning of making the right choice, because fear will paralyze you and keep you from walking in God's purpose for your life. When we planted Refuge Point Church, I was scared to death. So much so that I started second-guessing what God was calling me to do. Fear was telling me that we would never make it, that we would fail within a year, that we would never grow beyond 35 people, that I was going to bankrupt my savings account to keep it afloat, and on and on I could go. If I listened to the voice of fear, it would have caused me to doubt what God was calling me to do and miss the plan He had for me.

But thank God (in my churchy voice) that in my fear, He wasn't scared. If we are scared to do something that God is calling us to do, then maybe it should provide extra reassurance that He is calling us to do it. Don't fear what seems to be impossible – God is most likely involved in the process. It may seem absurd and impossible what God is calling you to, but with God, nothing is impossible.

In order to discuss how to gain wisdom, we must also discuss surefire ways to NOT gain wisdom. If I never exposed the killers of wisdom, then I am missing out on a crucial part of my job as a pastor. You can call me a screaming prophet if you want, but I am obligated to point out the foolish nature within all of us. So, today we are talking about something every American should be warned against – greed.

Greed is taking something for yourself that God never intended for you to have. Not only do we desire more wealth, but we are also greedy with our selfish desires. Think about how attractive a man becomes when he starts dating or gets married. Suddenly, all of the ladies want the former bachelor now that he's in a relationship. Why? Because things appear to be more attractive when they don't belong to us. Our culture justifies greed based on these instinctual desires. I want it – so it's mine! So many of us will make foolish decisions simply because we "want" something. This is how marital affairs begin and how money laundering begins. Wisdom, however, urges us to do the opposite. Wisdom says, "I want it, but it's not mine to have, so I'll be content and cultivate what I do have."

If greed makes you a fool, then generosity makes you wise. If greed brings death to situations, then generosity breathes life. Generosity says that everything I own isn't mine – I'm just managing the possessions God has granted me. This means the church I pastor isn't mine, my cars aren't mine, my money isn't mine, and my house isn't mine. Everything I own was given to me as a gift by God to build His kingdom.

Generosity does not beget stupid decisions and greed does not lead to smart ones. In what areas of your life is greed keeping you from living a wise life?

Ecclesiastes 7:9

Be not quick in your spirit to become angry, for anger lodges in the heart of fools.

The final killer of wisdom we are going to talk about is anger. Anger will destroy you and plant seeds of calamity in your life. Before we discuss the anger that leads to folly, you must know that there is a good kind of anger that all Christians should feel – anger toward things like poverty, sickness, injustice, and neglect of those who are struggling, such as orphans and refugees. This is a righteous anger that should lead us to action. And contrary to what many believe, it is very wise to be angry about what grieves the heart of God.

This is the anger that Jesus had when those on the fringes of society were wrongly treated. So, we should be angry that there are 400,000 orphans in the USA, or that 2.5 million Syrian refugee children have been displaced from their homes, and we should be enraged over the millions of aborted babies.

But the anger that leads to foolishness is not righteous. Have you ever been angry with someone? I've been so angry before that I thought fire was going to come out of my mouth. I have found that when we let unrighteous anger toward another person fester in our hearts, we become experts at pointing out the other person's weaknesses and become blind to their strengths. We begin to say things like, "You always do this" and "You never do that."

What we have done is taken our strengths, compared them to *their* weaknesses, thereby making a case for our anger. That's why we say and do things in our anger that we later regret. I can't say this enough about wisdom and folly, but I have never heard anyone say something out of anger that they later determined to be a wise.

I'll leave you with these three simple truths about anger: 1) Revenge is not for you to handle, 2) You have been forgiven by God – so you should forgive those who have made you angry, and 3) You are ambassadors of reconciliation. It is not God's design for you to walk in anger, but to walk in forgiveness and peace.

A Fight Club Ending?

As we approach the end of our study of Ecclesiastes, I hope
you haven't mentally checked out before we reach the final
lessons. Most of the time, we lose interest when we are reading
a story, not realizing that we'll miss the most important part –
the end. Think about if you read the Bible and never read
Revelation. You'd miss the parts about dragons being thrown
in lakes of fire, Jesus coming down with a tattoo, and a new
heaven and new earth! Seriously, think about if you watched
an M. Night Shyamalan film or Fight Club without watching
the end. You would miss the most important part! The same
goes for Ecclesiastes!

Up until now, we've had to deal with grumpy old Solomon,
but now he is happy Solomon so he ends this book on a
good note. Solomon has been telling us that our lives are
meaningless, how wisdom and folly are meaningless, how
wealth is meaningless, and how death is sure to come for all
of us. Who wants this guy at their dinner table? Not me. But
now, in a sudden plot twist, Solomon finds that with God at
the center of our lives, everything becomes meaningful. Life
does not have to be monotonous, but filled with challenging
situations from God. Wealth could actually be enjoyed if is
stewarded for God. If we follow God's wisdom, then we will
be less inclined to make foolish decisions. And the certainty
of death should make us enjoy life now and make the most
of it for God.

For ten chapters, Solomon has echoed the same refrain: life is meaningless! But thank God He didn't leave us to deal with the despair of life alone. We have a loving God who wants to bring us out of the meaninglessness of life and into a life filled with meaning and purpose.

44

Ecclesiastes 11:8-12:1

So if a person lives many years, let him rejoice in them all; but let him remember that the days of darkness will be many. All that comes is vanity. Rejoice, O young man, in your youth, and let your heart cheer you in the days of your youth. Walk in the ways of your heart and the sight of your eyes. But know that for all these things God will bring you into judgment. Remove vexation from your heart, and put away pain from your body, for youth and the dawn of life are vanity. Remember also your Creator in the days of your youth, before the evil days come and the years draw near of which you will say, "I have no pleasure in them"

So, in the end, Solomon tells us to pursue life and pursue God, but the truth is that most of the time there will be difficulties. Are you young? Then delight in the health and strength of your body. There's a whole world to be explored, and you have the strength to do it. *So you're telling me that we can actually enjoy and have meaning in this life?* Spoiler alert. Yes!

In verse 10, Solomon urges us to get rid of whatever causes "vexation," or offense, worry, or anxiety, in our lives. He addresses young people and says that while you are still youthful, get rid of your junk – or else it will haunt you the rest of your days. Your current issues will not disappear if you pretend they're not there. They become like the unwanted relative who is always showing up for the holidays. And the longer you wait or the older you get, the worse the offenses, or worries, or anxieties get. Remove these issues from your heart now.

So, how do we enjoy a meaningful life? Ecclesiastes 12:1 gives us the answer: don't forget Jesus and keep Him at the center of your life. At this point in the book, most people believe that Solomon was in his older years, so he felt the need to warn young people never to forget God. Don't wait until you get out of high school to get your life together. Don't wait until you get out of college to give your life to Jesus and don't wait until you're married or have kids. Do it now! While you are in your youth, keep Jesus at the center of your life. Don't wait until life slows down, because it never will! Consider Jesus now because you are not promised tomorrow. Keeping Christ at the center of your life is how we as followers of Jesus can enjoy and have a meaningful life.

45

Ecclesiastes 12:13-14

The end of the matter; all has been heard. Fear God and keep his commandments, for this is the whole duty of man. For God will bring every deed into judgment, with every secret thing, whether good or evil.

This whole book has led to the climax of Solomon's conclusion of his meaningless quest for a meaningful life. His experiment to find meaning under the sun led him to throw huge parties, empty vineyards for these parties, marry 700 women, hook up with 300 concubines, build forests, build countless houses, and his conclusion was that it was meaningless. After all was said and done, Solomon leaves us with two foundational truths – fear God and keep His commandments.

So what does it mean to fear God? Does this mean we are to fear God like we fear scary movies? Are we to fear God like children (and some adults) fear the bogeyman? Absolutely not! John Piper puts it like this: "The fear of God is the fear of straying from Him. Therefore it expresses itself in taking refuge in God." Anytime someone encountered God in the

Bible, they fell on their face. Not because God was scary, but because He demanded awe and respect. If I stand on the edge of the Grand Canyon, I'm going to be both scared and in awe. The awe is in its glory and beauty, and the fear comes from knowing what could happen if I take one more step. The awe, beauty, and majesty of the Grand Canyon draws nearly five million people to visit per year. That's what awe does– it draws you to the majestic power of God, knowing that He is going to take care of you.

The other truth that Solomon leaves us with is that we are to keep God's commandments. In other words, be obedient to what Jesus is telling you to do. This isn't delayed obedience, because delayed obedience is partial obedience and partial obedience is disobedience. When the Bible gives us clear commandments as believers, we are to follow them. Knowing that God loves us should lead us to obey His commandments, trusting that He is going to take care of us.

Once again, fear God and keep His commandments. When these two fundamental truths are applied to your life, you will begin to walk in a deeper level of what God has for you.

A Meaningful Benediction

I am convinced that the greatest need of humanity is not more stuff, bigger houses, a better looking spouse, more government, fancy cars, bold coffee or pumpkin spiced coffee, nice clothes, or hype-filled church experiences. Most of these things are good, but they are not what fills the emptiness of our souls. The greatest need of humanity can only be found over the sun.

When we realize that Jesus must be at the center of all of our activity, we will find purpose and a meaningful life. What unites us as followers of Christ is the Gospel of Jesus – the fundamental belief that Jesus is Lord. That is how we find meaning. We can strive for the things of this world, but what do we gain from that? It's simply meaningless.

My prayer and hope for the everyone is that we will echo Solomon's cry - that we will find our meaning and purpose in what is over the sun – Jesus Christ.

"The end of the matter; all has been heard. Fear God and keep his commandments, for this is the whole duty of man." – ~~Your~~ Eh hem...I mean, The Preacher

Notes

Day 9: John Ortberg, *The Me I want to Be: Becoming the Best Version of You.* (New York: Harper Collins, 2009).

Day 45: John Piper, "Afraid to Stray," Desiring God, April 20, 2012, https://www.desiringgod.org/articles/afraid-to-stray.

Printed in the United States
By Bookmasters